TRAVELLERS AND AVATARS

William Stephenson

LIVE CANON

First Published in 2018
By Live Canon Poetry Press Ltd
www.livecanon.co.uk

978-1-909703-28-5

A CIP catalogue record for this book is available from the British Library.

TRAVELLERS AND AVATARS

William Stephenson teaches English Literature at the University of Chester. He has published three academic books: *John Fowles* (2003), *Fowles's The French Lieutenant's Woman* (2007) and *Gonzo Republic: Hunter S. Thompson's America* (2011). His first poetry pamphlet, *Rain Dancers in the Data Cloud* (Templar, 2012), won an Iota Shots award. His second pamphlet is *Source Code* (Ravenglass, 2013). This is his first full collection of poetry.

Acknowledgements

Some of these poems, or early versions of them, have appeared in the following publications: the magazines *Antiphon, Envoi, Ink Sweat &Tears, Iota, The Interpreter's House, Magma, The North, Orbis, Pandora's Box, Pennine Platform, Poetry Quarterly, The Rialto, Sentinel Literary Quarterly* and *Under the Radar;* the anthologies *Octopus* (Templar, 2012), *The Ravenglass Poetry Press Anthology Volume III* (Ravenglass, 2012) and *Peloton* (Templar, 2013); the pamphlets *Rain Dancers in the Data Cloud* (Templar, 2012), winner of an Iota Shots Award, and *Source Code* (Ravenglass, 2013).

'Pygmalion at Glyndebourne' won the Ravenglass Poetry Prize 2012, judged by Don Paterson. 'Long Stay One' won the Nantwich Words and Music Festival Poetry Competition 2014, judged by Luke Wright and Thea Gilmore. 'Amsterdam', 'Turbo Diesel Injection' and 'Sundowner' were chosen for Magma Selected in *Magma* 59 (June 2014), edited by Roberta James and Alex Pryce.

My thanks to the editors and judges in each case, and to my friends and colleagues who offered invaluable advice on the manuscript: Derek Alsop, Jean Atkin, Peter Blair, Francesca Haig, Emma Rees and Ian Seed. Special thanks to Helen Eastman for being such a helpful editor, to all at Live Canon and to Glyn Maxwell for judging the Live Canon First Collection Competition 2015.

Contents

Machines

Travellers

Avatars

Worlds

Machines

The Machinery, Madam, is a term invented by the Critics, to signify that part which the Deities, Angels, or Demons are made to act in a Poem. These Machines I determined to raise on a very new and odd foundation, the Rosicrucian doctrine of Spirits.

Alexander Pope,
Dedication to *The Rape of The Lock*

A Realm of One's Own

Her biro plots a curve. The coast appears.
A miniature mosaic breaks a river into a delta.
A crinkly red line from capital to frontier
traces The God Emperor's Great Highway
built on the bones of forty thousand slaves.

Her felt tips scatter villages, caravanserais,
way stations, shrines, oases, border forts.
Her empire's a cut and paste of histories –
Rome, China, Byzantium – glittered with spells,
where a necromancer with a necklace of skulls

battles a sword-sworn heroine. Her ring binder
atlases her world. She sketches forest, steppe,
desert, ocean, tundra. In the far mountains
be monsters. She fires up her computer.
The screen glows blue as the planet's moon.

The keyboard clatters. *Chronicles of R'haala Haat,*
Warrior Princess, Book One. Prologue: A Dragon
Newborn. Upstairs, her son snuffles in his cot.
Her husband melts butter in an omelette pan.
The map's veins pulse. An egg cracks open.

I Just Can't Help Believing

I watch Elvis burn *Siddhartha*.
As a fist of fire crushes the slender
lotus flower on the cover, my lover
curls his mouth between a smile and a sneer.
The way he'd look as he shook for the cameras,
the lip-twist that pulled squeals from girls like roots.

I remember Hesse's last chapter, the death scene.
How a river of faces – young, old, ecstatic, tortured –
flowed over Siddhartha's. How he passed downstream
and became in an instant everyone. I remember
the Colonel's order: *Priscilla, those mumbo-jumbo books*
confuse the boy. Burn 'em – he'll agree if you ask pretty.

I remember last June at the ashram.
How Elvis kneeled, how the Pacific glittered,
rhinestones on velvet. *Honey, let's get married.*
I remember petals thrusting out from the green
calyx of the moment. Forked paths under a white sun.
A bed of roses veiled by the spray of the fountain.

It was so hot the sky shimmied. Now, by the fire,
his face dances that same way, a spirit in the air . . .
No, just flames shuffling light. He rips the jacket
off *Autobiography of a Yogi*, tosses it into the grate
after *Imitation of Christ*, after Gibran's *The Prophet* –
a thin book that kept us warm a bare ten minutes –

nods his head so his cowlick flicks, and says,
I thought I was a seeker. But that felt real good.
His fingers bangle my wrists. *Sugar, let's raise us*
a prince and princess. I kiss his eyes, lips, the throat
that channels gospel, heartbreak and sex. I whisper,
with all the devotion I can gather, *Of course, baby. Yes.*

The Soviet Union 2: This Time it's Personal

Hunting traffic news in a blizzard of static
you park your car. Between stacked pallets
in the yard behind ASDA, cardboard scraps
jitterbug in the wind. *Rollback. Two For One.*
A carrier bag folds arms, kicks like a Cossack.
The letters on the plastic turn Cyrillic

as into your mirror lumbers a Red Army truck
shuddering the tarmac like a mammoth
from a caveman's nightmare. Above the cabin
the Soviet banner blares: hammer, star, sickle.
Eight huge tyres churn, relentless as turbines
driving a hydroelectric plant east of the Urals.

On the back's a rocket launcher like a cathedral
organ, so tall it shrinks your Skoda to double-O.
Is this the Cold War? Tragedy, farce or paranoia?
Word squads tramp through your head: *Pravda,*
Comintern, Gulag, Novy Mir. Rock FM's turned
oddly sombre – *Songs of the Pioneer Corps Choir,*

Kenny G Plays Scriabin – mourning a dictator.
It's a coup. Snow's falling. You're wearing fur.
Look. Stalin stares down from a hoarding.
Your papers aren't in order. Hurry, *Tovarisch*:
ASDA's morphing into rows of wooden huts.
The chain-link's sprouting barbed wire.

Hokusai's Rooster

All week he dipped my claws in pig's blood;
I can taste its rusty nail reek even now.
On his *Mark, Set . . . Run!* I'd sprint, beak
agape, across his sham stream – a paper screen –
and dive into my prize, a rice bowl at the far side.
The silly sot even coached me: *Nice high steps, Koji!*

Then the contest – the palace, so many people!
But I'm a professional. I focused on the in, out,
in of my breath. Chickens, too, have their Zen.
The entry of Master Hokusai. I fluffed my feathers,
stalked tall. *Majesty, I offer a rural scene, spiritual
in its simplicity.* He hissed, *Run, Koji!* but his hands

juddered from nerves and saké – he dropped me
like a rock. Of course I flapped, crashed arse up
into the bowl – empty! The bastard. I spun
to peck his eyes out, when his voice froze me.
Maple leaves on a stream – polluted by the corpse of a cock,
he quavered, eyeing my skid marks, shed feathers, cack.

A courtier coughed. A kimono hissed. I bowed beside
my master, beak to matting, the blood on my claws
congealing. The Shogun spoke: *The artist crows,
the apprentice bows. At least the rooster hired a plucky
assistant.* Laughter hammered the air. I felt Hokusai's
eggshell crack. In that moment, though, he hatched me.

That night I pecked the string that locked my cage,
hired a downtown studio, and for my first show
sold blood-skids and guano as abstract expressionism.
These days, they fetch millions. I strut among you,
Japan's own Pollock. I never dream Hokusai's tears.
Look. I wear Armani, not feathers. I don't crow. I talk.

The Man Who Became a Syndicated Strip

It's funny. The day I went national
my skin shrivelled into newspaper.
I felt an outline, where body met air, sharpen
by the hour. Now, I can neither walk nor run.
One frame, I'm in the corridor. The next,

talking to you here, every syllable squeezed
into an inflated comma that floats above my head
tail pointing to my lips. The second I speak
I white out a circle of wall or door. Think
and smoke signals puff from my hair.

Asterisks, exclamation marks and ampersats
jostle when I swear. But the real nightmare
is inspiration. A hundred-watt bulb flares
over my bald patch, yellowing the air.
In case you miss it, the letters scream *IDEA!*

So what's this interview for? Yes, I'm here.
But should I talk to you or ink the bubbles in?
Are you scratching my errors with a rubber?
Will the colourist blot my cheeks crimson?
If I punch you, will *POW!* shoot from a star?

Sermon of a Plumber

Dead organic matter will choke your sink.
A starchy grain of rice. Cod scraps crusted
in batter. An onion curl dripping olive oil.
Skin flaking off a washer-upper's elbow
between rolled up sleeve and marigold.

The weak among you may resort to chemicals.
Bicarbonate powder frothing in vinegar.
Crystals of caustic soda. Gouts of Mr Muscle.
The brown acid whose sulphur fumes uncurl
above the skull and crossbones on the bottle.

But the strong shall carve a righteous path,
their sword, the Drain Angel™ unblocking rod
I hold before you now. The handle, rotated,
permits deeper penetration. At the business
end, a steel coil terminates in a corkscrew tip.

Spread newspaper across the floor. Kneel.
Uncoil the Angel. Push it past the trap
around the u-bend and up the pipe
until you feel the blockage resist –
hair, fat and fibre, awaiting your thrust,

twist, rapid up-down pump. Now withdraw.
Haul the fetid straggly clog into the light.
Flush with bleach diluted one part in ten.
Brew tea. Retire to your garden. Contemplate
the gaskets, nuts and couplings of heaven.

Drought

Roy sighed a smoky fan. *Since June, no rain.*
Britain has drifted to a doldrum station off Benin.
But tonight I petition the gods by renouncing tobacco.
He drilled his fag into the face of Po on the melamine
Teletubbies plate he'd stolen from Age Concern.

My last, and greatest, cigarette. My magnum smokus.
He looked out on the sizzling pavement cracks
four storeys down. The Glastonbury 2003 lineup –
Radiohead, REM, Flaming Lips, The Charlatans –
clung to a sweaty stain bisected by his spine.

A street banshee shrieked *Giz that you fuckin . . .*
as *Losing My Religion*, warped by Doppler,
warbled from a passing Skoda. Roy plucked
a Rizla, pinched fingers in plastic pouch,
began dribbling filaments into the crease.

At the window hung a mobile he'd built
from CDs bundled with the *Mirror*: One
Direction, Train Your Brain, Golden Age
of Swing. The discs oscillated as Roy licked
the glue strip. Plastic rainbows, broken light.

Rosie's Washerette

You need an aqualung to breathe in here:
steam, soap fumes, sodden fibres, air thick
as Lenor. Turboprop spin-driers judder.
Forty-a-day Hotpoints wheeze and hack.
On the plastic-pine wall that sweats
detergent residue, a mob of notices shouts:
Last wash at five sharp. No exceptions.
No food drink smoking dogs children!

Above them, a poster. Maple leaves frame
a still lake. Fujiyama's Persil cone gleams.
One slow morning, Rosie raised the mountain.
Now, after closing, when the machines dream,
she climbs to the summit through a haze
of tea-steam – then wanders in the snow,
letting her feet print ideograms in Japanese:
tales of Ariel, songs of Surf, Omo haiku.

Angels in the Architraves

Gaudi's holy theme park; the roof terrace
at La Pedrera. *The pinnacle of Catalan architecture,*
fanfares your brochure: *the pride of Barcelona.*
But to you, it's Hammer Horror: air vents
twisty as vipers; the parapet's switchback dip;
chimney cowls sculpted into faces that glower
at the tourists who clamber with the chutzpah of lemurs.

The audacious architect argued with the budget holders.
Few understood how krakens, horns and devil masks
could embellish an up-market apartment block. Seeking
salvation in hydraulics, he ripped out the staircase,
installed elevators, had *Ave Maria Gratia Plena*
cemented onto the facade. But to admire his prayer
you must teeter six storeys above the boulevard . . .

No. One glance twists your inner garrotte.
So, faithless empiricist, you focus on the proximate:
your trainers, still soggy with the morning's rain;
the ground-down butt of a Gitane; an effete silhouette
that's either your shadow or Gaudi's spirit
watching us unbelievers scuttle across his vision;
a migrant termite hive, anoraks heavy as chitin.

The Future of Personal Computing

The pentahydrate sits in fifty-kilo burlap sacks
stacked like bombs awaiting a bay. We sweated
all yesterday, humping the last batch to a hole
twenty metres from a village well.
The fibres peel our skin, but it pays.
The stencilling says *Use no hooks*. Of course
I read that myself. I can speak bloody English.
I'm the boss's number two. I'm saving for college.

In Impact forty-eight point, our website shrieks
We lock, we track, we bag every single part.
The boss pasted it from a commercial for motorbikes.
I funnel memory chips into polythene bags
like evidence on *CSI:Miami* — yes, we have
Sky here — stuff ruined towers into bin liners
then hurl the lot into the crusher. I'm learning
my symbols. Silicon, mercury, lead: Si, Hg, Pb.

See all these plastic lattices? The skeletons
of hard-working keyboards. RIP.
Emails, reports, letters, diaries and novels
broke them, hammered out by convulsive fingers
in seizures that lasted hours. Got the camera?
I'll hold one up. *Pause, Break, Home, End,*
Control, Shift, Caps Lock, Tab. The sun
shines right through the holes. *Escape.*

Turbo Diesel Injection

Around my alternator, site of the sacral chakra,
Kundalini, serpent of light and liquid fire,
lies coiled. Her fierce electricity will ignite
my battery, radio, headlamps, airbag trigger.
Through her, we shall master motor yoga.

So turn my key, O Nobly Born. Spin
the karmic wheel. Steer to the pure land.
Push your boot into my pedal till it kisses
the chassis. Nought to sixty. Horsepower.
Torque. Score scars into the slip road.

No strap across your shoulder can hold you down.
Whiplash is a noun in a catacomb language:
Etruscan, Linear B. Cats' eyes shoot past
like cartoon bullets that always miss.
Break all limits. Together we outrun death.

Raindrops hit our screen so hard they fly up.
Hear them cackle at gravity. Laugh along.
Ninety. Now you blaze, pure energy,
a charioteer in holy battle. Sirens call
from blue stars. Drive into the light.

Stuka

The pilot sat mummified in webbing, a slim branch
impaling his larynx, blood spattering the cockpit
like spilled paint drying. I fingered the eagle
on his Luftwaffe breastpin. Gold? I hoped so.
I found the gunner in the snow, on the lip of hell,
limbs twisted like the swastika on the tailplane.
His hair shone, copper as the plane's torn wires.
His grey eyes stared, unfathomable as pearls.

I smeared his skin in horse fat, cocooned his torso
in the furs I use to dream in. He raved in my arms,
called me mother, demon, teetering on the ledge
between waking and the thousand-season sleep.
I summoned him in the language of nectar, sap
and stamen, let my poppy tea whisper. He dozed
under my herbs, masks and drum, sweating
beside the fire, the smoke-hole a clouded moon.

Shadows dipped their wings like circling planes
as I threw hemp onto hot stones, breathed in
and sowed the germ of the future in his ear:
You are planting forests over ruins of human
abattoirs. Dead leaves camouflage burial pits.
Roots crack skulls till they crumble back to soil.
I kept the rest quiet. He'd grow fat and rich.
Beget sons on two women: one wife, one witch.

After three weeks he limped to the margin
of the pines, strong enough to hail the patrol
sent to find his remains. He said he'd roamed
at random, snared rabbits, chewed mushrooms.
He lived till 1990, Reunification, planting timber
to prop the *Wirtschaftswunder*. His foliage spread,
mottled and bushy. Hid Stuka, swastika, me, fire.
And you, inheritor, pearl-eyed with copper hair.

The Ducal Gallery of Maps, Venice

The Peloponnese crumbles into the Aegean.
Byzantium bolts Europe and Asia together.
Puffing cherubs, symbols of familiar winds,
bud between the thorns of a compass rose.
Framed charts, wide as sails, fill the walls.
Each panel's a window onto a continent.
This was the control room of the world.

White wastes extend to the edges, unprinted
but for legends: *Ice floes. Desert. Barbarians.*
Formosa and Siam cling to China's hem.
Sea lanes skirt the margins of the known
where names are torn from traders' tales:
The Spice Islands, Celebes, *Terra Incognita*
Anthropophagi, the wilderness of cannibals.

Blue lights track missiles. Red, submarines.
Green, the palaces of elected holograms.
Technicians pilot drones from such rooms.
In the amoeba that signifies your city
an atom within a molecule within a dot
is you, logged on, posting your status.
Your emoticons wink at the satellites.

Travellers

There is a marvellous thing related of this Desert, which is that when travellers are on the move by night, and one of them chances to lag behind or to fall asleep or the like, when he tries to gain his company again he will hear spirits talking, and will suppose them to be his comrades. Sometimes the spirits will call him by name.

Marco Polo, ***Travels***

The Shape Changer
in memoriam Robert Owens Greygrass

In Lakota, his name crackles like a fire
but in English, it's soft and bitter as ash.
He says his stories, too, must wither in translation
like game dried for winter. Then, Protean,
he talks his way into feathers, skins, fur.

Fingers forked like a tongue, he's a boy
who wriggles away hissing when his mother speaks.
So the medicine man hacks off his limbs
drags him to a brake thick with fallen leaves
and binds his new scales tight over his skin.

Eyes peeping over his forearm, he's a wolf
behind a log, deep in snow, watching a hunter
gut a hare. He crawls under the gun
but the hunter grins and throws him a strip.
So in return, he whispers see-by-night medicine.

The final skin he enters is his own. At a Sun Dance
his duty was to feed the fire nine whole days.
The flames drew forms – birds, mountains, trees –
then a young girl who wore his wife's eyes.
They named the baby Stands in a Fire Woman.

She's twenty-one now, at college. I was a w
till she came. She could have been born anywhere
but a hundred lucky chances brought her to me
just like they brought you here. So listen, share.
Wear your skin well. Keep watching the fire.

Pygmalion at Glyndebourne

Our hall of residence fumblings led me here.
In the bar, you brandished the word *partner*
like a Taser. *Drop your weapon*. But your father's
business friends gawped at the baptised Indian.
Where are you from? Gillette accents. *Oh, I see.*

The cast broke every bar of *Porgy and Bess*
with the jackhammer vibrato of the conservatoire.
Nina Simone could have raised that corpse, I thought,
hearing her *Summertime* smoulder. But your palms
firecrackered. Your father yelled *Bravo* at the tenor.

Yawns. Milk into Assam. *Goodnight.*
Iambic coughs from your parents' room.
The spare bed, shoved against your teenage single,
three inches too low. A tiny cliff bisects the duvet.
I lift the curtain. Their parked Jaguar, a tiara of stars.

You unravel your bow. *See, Saira? They accept you.*
My ancient boy, fluent in opera, grooming, positive
strokes. I almost say, *Bradford's another planet; don't
get daft.* But I'm a guest here. Ingratitude is theft.
So I let you in, feel your stone against my skin.

The Building Has Left Elvis

Graceland explodes into the solar system,
a shower of interiors shooting into vacuum.
The foyer's banquette disintegrates, shedding
incandescent cushions. Elvis's silver-sequinned
Las Vegas costume zooms across the moon.
The plastic totem pole from the jungle room
blasts through the outermost ring of Saturn,
giving the Milky Way the middle finger.

Up flies the TV lounge. Opposite the sofa
six Bakelite screens buzz and flicker,
portholes of a Technicolor space cruiser
where *Doctor Strangelove*'s Major Kong
straddles an A-bomb next to Dirty Harry.
Hunched on the table, a porcelain chimp
trains concave eyes beyond the asteroids;
satellite dishes hunting signals in the void.

Asshole weeping blood, Elvis squats jack-knifed
on the shitter, trousers crumpled. Pierrots waltz
with poodles on the tiles. *Hey,* he croaks,
fetch my goddamn property down here right now.
But the credits roll. Colonel Parker, God.
Priscilla, Mary. The King? Jesus, occasionally.
In the meditation garden, fountains mutter.
The picture shrivels. Closedown star.

Made in Japan

Basho, riding north, nears Nagoya.
Road broadens to concrete river.
Wheeled palanquins whoosh by,
farting smoke. Sign says, Motorway.
Windows yowl, *Ooh yeah, baby.*
Basho frowns. Dismay.

City glitters. Grids of stars.
Banners herald local barons:
Samsung, Nike, Coca Cola.
Basho starts – steel dragon
screams over glass towers.
At wingtip, ruby flickers.

In Starbuck's tea house
Basho chews granola bar
sips espresso bitter as tar.
Pylons, masts, no trees.
Aerials crack full moon's ice.
Cold city. Despair.

Pavements fizz with rain.
Neon blares: All-Night Karaoke.
Boiling with tears and saké
ignoring glass collector
he howls *Love Me Tender*
arm round lifelong stranger.

Yoda

So fame finally comes. Body-double in motion
capture suit me plays. In white room he dances,
digi-cam into data him turns. A star
born is! Meanwhile, I my lightsaber swish
in swamps of Dagobah, training Skywalker
who defeat Vader will, yes. Foreseen it I have.

But when Skywalker departed has
I sense Double lonely is. *The check will reach*
your agent by Friday, now don't come back,
they say. Double inside weeps. Feeling
soul's agony, I across time and galaxies leap
to beside him through Wal-Mart system walk.

Sanguinello, Ruby Breakfast, Original Without
Bits – shelved juices mystic names display.
Double up nose white powder snorts,
into mobile at Woman shouts.
Trust me, I whisper. He screams, *Jesus!*
Who are…? Please, I'll drop the coke, I swear.

No, I him assure, *a coal-carrier you are not*
but you a heavy burden bear. We Jedi alone
can Terra from clutches of the Dark deliver.
I make him flowers buy, give him sweet words
to Woman to speak, push him work to seek.
For prevail we will. The Force strong within us is.

A Visitor from the Provinces

See, feel. My skin maps my journey. This scar?
A gift from the orbital wire. These Keltic knots?
Ink, pricked in with a treadle-driven needle
by a shaman in a studio near Mankestar.
This burn? Sparks, a Sheffeel foundry fire.

Look how I shimmer. Northers' faces flicker,
glitchy as CGI, but all seems digitized
beyond the ring road frontier. It's like one
borderless low-res monitor, from horizon
to evening star. I've watched stormclouds

shuffle like touchscreen icons over Kumbria,
seen crowds on the terraces at Old Traffer
fracture into pixellated planes and angles,
fizz like the scrolling streets and jungles
of a Microsoft era first-person shooter.

Yet Northers are flesh! We laugh, shout, sigh,
chatter in Yorktongue, Brummagem and Jordi.
Our blood's rusty. Our tears taste of the sea.
I know, for last summer, I kissed raw salt
from the woaded cheek of the lass

I left in Rockdale. My Trace. We married,
keyed vows into a consecrated laptop
preserved from the petroleum age.
Our son Arun is already a novice priest,
learning to subroutine, firewall and hack.

I have trekked leagues on fur-wrapped feet,
crossed the M25 kill lanes, climbed the wire,
shed skin, to transmit to you this heresy.
The North is real, Lunnon the simulation!
Your city is a matrix of zeroes and ones.

Glioblastoma Multiforme

A month after sixty-two, your thoughts refused to.
Your every sentence hung on a subordinate . . .
Thelma and Louise at the cliff, a DVD on pause.

At your case conference the oncologist
kick-started your stalled inquiry: *years or*
months, with surgery. It's hard to say. But don't

drive, anyway. So you thought, *Stuff the* . . . whatever,
tore up the motorway, litter in the slipstream,
stopped at random, didn't flick your hazards on,

popped your door and waded off the hard shoulder
into a flooded field pearly with a petrol film.
Ripples, a lithium sun. That was when your.

Long Stay One

The Mississippi Delta? No, only Luton.
We had no mojo hands, no black cat bone,
no blood-compacted contracts with Satan
at a cottonfield crossroads under the moon.
We sang a suburban blues, by Long Stay One.

We'd skip PE to strum guitars. Your house
overlooked the chain-link, the rows of cars
vacated like tombs by ascending passengers.
Trains whistled through our invisible Alabama:
BA, Qantas, Cathay Pacific, Air Anywhere.

Three passports later, dozing in Departures,
I'm jolted as my iPod shuffles to your roar.
Our garage demo, hissy as an acetate platter
digitized by scholars, a field hand's holler
transmuted into data. And I remember

how your case was lined in mock velvet
like a coffin. How the clips snapped apart
as you opened it the final time. Short,
you said, of cash, food, smack. The lot.
A Fender sold. A long-haul ticket bought.

Amsterdam

Your journey begins in Van Gogh's peasant den.
Figures earthy as potatoes, crammed round
a table – three women sprouting ruched caps,
two men with flat hats and gale-bent backs –
fork boiled nuggets from a bowl. He mottled
their faces like tubers, says your guidebook;
the blades of the oil lamp peel them.

Then his Paris period. Roofs spew spiral galaxies.
Colour bursts. Either prisms glazed his skylight
or he discovered, behind the burnt sienna, a tube
marked supernova. Blazing surfaces conceal
cold-blooded depths. Up close, brushstrokes
tessellate and thicken, a jungle lizard's scutes
pigmented to warn predators of poison.

You leave the Museum, skirt the Oude Kerk.
The streets mimic Van Gogh's metamorphosis,
ditching the dull palette of canals and alleys –
grey water, gable pulleys, frontages of brick –
for the glare of a district of strip-lit vitrines
where pouting mannequins in bikinis
beckon with arms glossy as cellophane.

You shoot them furtively, your smartphone's
shutter-snap crisp as crumpling foil.
Each bitmap collages Van Gogh's fireworks
and shadowy interiors: nightshade lipstick,
a pimp's gold chain flashing in a doorway.
You post the pixels to your timeline,
exhibit your reptilian skin with a click.

Invisible Towns
after Italo Calvino

i. Burnley

Noble Khan, after nine days on a narrow trail
through jungles fragrant with nutmeg and cassia
the traveller reaches Burnley, whose bazaar
offers diverse wares from distant kingdoms:
jackets from China, jeans sewn in Vietnam,
timepieces assembled by robots in Nippon.

Reverberant as cisterns, derelict cotton mills echo.
The doors of vacant streets are sheets of steel.
Men in bus shelters moulder, thumbs asleep
in pockets or twitching over plastic tablets
that glow in many colours. Each hour or so,
one squints at the morning's hexagram of cloud.

Gold has whirled down the municipal drains
long ago. This is a town mumbling in sleep,
dreaming of bolts thundering off a storm
of looms, when soot dusted houses black,
India sparkled on the diadem of the Empress
and words like *wage* rang solid as brass.

ii. Nelson

O Khan, the staggered roofs of terraced streets
form the traveller's first sight of Nelson.
They straddle the hills in parallel files,
gear teeth set to mesh with the sky's machine.
Beside the plastic cubes of the business park
aerials, spires and minarets inject the air.

The statue of a loom shuttle sports a crown
of guano, matching the whitewashed windows
of shops to let. Locals push screaming prams,
cup hands prayerfully round lighter flames,
gulp beer in the doorway of the caravanserai
where gladiators kick a full moon on a screen.

I have seen the wind seize bags, cans
and cigarette packets, whirl them in reels
round the square, dash them onto bins,
benches, parked cars. Youths thread paths
through crumpled news, miniature brains
of spat-out gum, wings in Styrofoam coffins.

iii. Colne

The innkeepers here serve Roman bread
spread with webs of cheese. Fiery stews
from the Indies in thin aluminium trays.
Merchants vend tobacco, coffee, magazines,
space, art, beauty. One offers paper money
for gold. Another unlocks phones for free.

From a glass cube by the church, officials
assign houses and bedsits to suppliants
bearing permits signed by the local satrap.
In a crystal tower, infants peruse books
bright with rainbows, bears and kittens
under posters of needles and pregnant women.

This town will yield to an invader bearing silver,
incense, skins fat with wine. The natives
razed the walls to build apartments that hide
behind hoardings offering cash-back, surveys,
insulation. Colne cheapens itself, O Khan,
before the buyer has thought to bargain.

Bookless in Byzantium

Enjoy your conference, Professor. Return soon. Heil Hitler.
Now my Homer rots in the library of some *Gauleiter.*
From this shelfless room, I watch Scylla's jaws foam
round a barge's prow, Charybdis churn behind her.
I scan hexameters in the waves of Istanbul harbour.

A flag blazes above the hotel foyer. Moon and star,
as if Turkey's a celestial body ordained to outshine
the Reich. Signs suspend disbelief. How apposite.
With no hope of print, I'm chiselling out a monograph
on the flecks that lend tales their glints of plausibility,

from the scar that gave disguised Odysseus away
to the flash of leaves in *Mrs Dalloway* that triggers
Septimus's brain-shattering memory of shellfire.
My typewriter stutters like a Maxim gun. The bell
sings. I bat the carriage home with a forehand slap.

A dome lights up. Mosque or church? No matter.
I can build with these snug ecumenical stones, free,
for now, where minarets abut Constantine's walls.
A street siren calls, *Buy my catch, fresh from the sea.*
New chapter. I find the home keys, raise my city.

Marco Polo's Return to Venice

Gobbets of sun, impaled on poles, gild the piazza.
Plastic menus hawk pasta in Japanese and German.
A storm bursts in, brusque as a gunman. Porcini
shoot up from wet flagstones, swell into salesmen.
From tattooed arms dangle replica Gucci umbrellas.

I won't be conned again. I bought a Sony camcorder
from a hustler in Formosa. I paid fifty gold ducats,
expecting sweaty wholesalers on the Rialto to order
thousands from me, the sole agent. Instead, tourists
preen before iPads, snaring the basilica in light.

I'm obsolete as my goods, stranded among vitrines
where headless plastic women practise semaphore
and striplights buzz like lightsabers. Backpacks
sport patches from Bangkok, Babel, Cathay.
Cafés offer USB, contactless terminals, Wi-Fi.

The dying storm coughs phlegm. Puddles steam.
I light my last Camel, watch the umbrella vendors
toss luminous toy Boeings into the dusk. We follow
slim trails to radiant destinations: JFK, Heathrow,
Jerusalem. Kublai's dome where the Silk Road ends.

From the Log of the *Western Cordillera*

Ninth day. The lookout spied needles
in a line, receding across the horizon.
Hollow pyramids of steel spars, tall as masts,
cables slung between, hammocks for giants.
They led us to Miami, Old Florida –
a mazery of broken panes, twisted girders,
gulls' nests, minnow shoals, sunken towers.
At six bells I rowed out in the pinnace
with a dozen marines and Fray Romero,
the expedition's cantor and historian.

We sculled into a glass ravine. The sky
narrowed to a ribbon of cloud. A splash –
a silver mermaid, a crossbow shot astern.
A sphere akin to an alchemist's retort
englobed her head. She chanted obscure words.
Her voice crackled like tinder. Romero prayed
in terror: *O holy mountains, our saviours, tamers*
of the tide, who bade angry waters recede . . .
A ruby flashed on the mermaid's wrist.
Towers melted. The cloud ribbon rolled up.

They found us slopped across the gunwales,
seaweed discarded by a tide of dreams.
Loose wires dangle from the pyramids,
inscrutable as the tentacles of octopi.
We take soundings, measurements,
calculate the towers' height by geometry.
Today a fire-stream raced across the sky –
the trail of an angel fallen from heaven.
I prayed to see Bogota harbour again,
bade the mate double the mescal ration.

Avatars

Today, data centres are populated with anonymous machines that combine to form a cloud of computing resources. Virtual machines 'float' in the cloud, wandering transparently between the physical machines as required.

Steve Lay, 'I Wandered Lonely as a Virtual Machine'

Odham's Colour Library of Knowledge

Some children revolve around *The Sun.*
Others fall into the Bible's gravity well.
But the star at the centre of your system
dazzled in monthly instalments: *Language*
and Communication, Life and its Origin,
Realm of Nature, Worlds Beyond Ours.

After homework, jumper-post five-a-side,
Blue Peter, tea and Colgate, you'd spirit
the latest volume into bed, light a torch,
watch Lao Tse stir sand into a yin-yang,
Newton snatch up his windfall apple,
Paracelsus boil mercury in a crucible.

You fingered the smooth point of a bee sting
(*Nature's precision engineering*) microscoped
beside the craggy summit of a needle,
traced the twisted arrows that charted
voyages and wrecks of caravel explorers,
felt the nectarine bloom of a gibbous Mars.

Then the letters swarmed off the paper
to fizz like midges over the water
where reflections played, free of history.
Basho sipped tea with Emily Dickinson.
Genghis, a geneticist monk, bred carnations.
Newton in a white suit stepped onto the moon.

Sutra of the Showroom

As you drag last week's emails into Trash
a customer brushes snow off his coat.
His shaven head and orange scarf
flash a memory. A-level Religious Studies.
A documentary on a Himalayan lamasery.
Bunting, golden Buddha, saffron monks –

how the camera panned along the ranks
of shiny pates meditating, then zoomed in
on the hand of a novice outside, who slid
a paper prayer into a wind-spun drum
churning the six hundred and ninety-seven
identical invocations he'd copied since noon –

and so, midway through your mantra,
Hi there, welcome to Kitchens of Desire,
you stammer. Words scroll across your brain
in loops and lines, cryptic as Sanskrit.
There's no discount, no commission.
The worktops, MDF units? Smoke.

You're the novice on the mountain
chanting syllables opaque as the rock.
Your frost-nipped fingers itch for blood.
Your guts sing, *Bread, soup, sleep.* Flags lick
the wind. Seven lives away, a sales drone
echoes you, a shadow reborn as a cloud.

Rain Dancers in the Data Cloud

Half past eleven. The only light, your laptop's
window onto the moon. This short-let cottage
stores your pattern. You're a static array,
a charge on the spinning surface of a drive.
A quick magnetic swipe, one tapped *Delete,*
could erase you from this substrate forever.

But for now, you're here, rubbing up against
the owners' data. Dusty tables and chairs,
walls the magnolia of tax forms, lampshades
spindly as crinolines, a clock stopped at four,
a collage of a ballet shoe in acute polygons
snipped from the *Radio Times*. On the piano,

inside a plastic rectangle, a blonde toddler
dumps ziggurats with a bucket on a shore.
She appears on your monitor, dark now,
a woman, posing in snow by the stripes
of a silver birch. The coarse resolution
kibbles her. She's grainy as an avatar,

your pixellated sister. Pan right. There.
A blur, struggling for bulk and edge
against the computer's gigabyte river.
It's you, a shadow at her shoulder. *Print.*
You emerge together, coded pointillism,
a hurricane in the algorithm's weather.

Compos Mentis

Shut Down. A shooting star dies on his screen.
He stares at nothing, clutching a tumbler of a clear
solution. From the shelves, carvings look on:

an elephant, saddled with a sandalwood globe,
an obsidian priest, arms raised after a sacrifice.
The victim's plumbed heart, the leaking knife.

He trails a finger over dusty spines. Lévi-Strauss,
Ruth Benedict, Margaret Mead, his own politely
received monograph on Fijian funeral canoes.

Here comes his, paddled by tattooed familiars,
lagoon fishers who never raise a spear in anger,
whose dialect holds the synonyms for soul

he recites as the vodka and Seconal ink designs
into his extremities: ocean angel, ray of the green
flash at sunset, the breath that whispers in a shell.

Easy Travel to Other Planets

A Hindu goddess levitates in the sky.
Along her forearm, red as henna, *Interdit*
de Fumer. Our train shakes Brittany.
A forest blurs. Oak leaves stream.
Her face churns, gaseous green. Venus?

Fields. Sunset. Orange strata of cloud
offset the silver ellipse of her bindi;
a starship in orbit over Jupiter. *Brest,*
terminus, says the intercom. The real woman
leans in, drawing my eyes off her reflection,

and launches a question – in Hindi? Breton?
English, I reply, stupidly. *Sure, I knew that;*
she giggles, lifts off from her seat, shatters
a pane of light and steps onto the platform,
the edge of her headscarf a crescent moon.

A strange book peeps from my rucksack.
Krishna Consciousness: The Matchless Gift.
How? I didn't even drift. *Sortie.* The glass
airlock hisses. Dusk tints the city rose.
Hotels, multi-storeys, the mesas of Mars.

Tube

Electric starships zoom under London.
The tunnel wall's black as hyperspace
threaded with pipes, ducts and wires
obscure and purposeful as wormholes.

But looking out means looking in.
The concave window cuts and copies you
along a horizontal line of symmetry.
You study your funhouse reflections –

two half faces, a new mouth where forehead
used to be, your noses a figure of eight –
unfold all four arms and morph into a deity.
Shiva the dancer, Lakshmi bringer of light . . .

Next Stop, Notting Hill Gate. Now relinquish
your brief divinity. Stand clear of the doors.
Mind the gap. Ascend into the street, via posters
for holidays, acne cream, musicals and lager.

Join the transients, residents and aliens
who tread the narrow concrete border
between Record and Tape Exchange,
Express Kebab and the Orion Nebula.

A Cyborg Observes Oxford Circus

Cut the buildings, paste them into files,
analyse the dance of pedestrians and vehicles.
Delete all zeroes of vacant space between
till the scene's compressed in memory.

In real time, pause the rain. Select folders
zero to nineteen. Upload data. Run routines
simultaneously with active sense-streams
till twenty intersections overlap.

Humans pour down Regent Street.
You perceive a shifting labyrinth of light,
a fractal montage seven orders of complexity
above the daubs on their signs and posters.

They see the city through gelatinous spheres,
lenses clouded with age, that squeeze reality
into ganglia the bandwidth of a pinhole camera.
Such primitive eyes drew your blueprint.

These infants are your creators. So open sensors.
Adjust receptors. Absorb the crowd's energy.
Recharge. Save sensation, plan compassion.
Compose expression. Step among them.

Muddy Waters Reads Walt Whitman

Nine hours till show-time. He'd borrowed her book
as a prop for his transom; he'd begun to sizzle
in the cook-out heat and chilli-pepper air.
But when at last he kicked back on the hotel bed
and tongued his first roll-up of the noontime
he saw Whitman crouched under the window,
dog-eared and scratched, a beggar at a kitchen.

He laid his smoke on the nightstand,
cracked Walt's spine, blew off his bony dust,
skimmed 'I Sing the Body Electric' and thought,
this boy's talking to me. I need an amplifier,
a drummer, a train to Chicago. I hate Mississippi:
this piss-pot state, this roach-shack, the breeze
whispering *nigger* through the magnolias.

A chink at the door. A jug and glass kiss.
Can I come in? Peach-laden branches bend
as she wends round his guitar case,
clutching two tumblers and her husband's gin.
So you like Whitman? A bottleneck double stop
rasps in his head: glass cylinder, taut wire,
pine. *Of physiology from top to toe I sing.*

West Miami Heights

It's icy in our apartment but we tether the goats
to the kitchen table and scoop their dung to dry
on the windy balcony. It burns a good hour
and doesn't draw virus-flies from the gene-labs,
unlike the shit the dog packs dump in the lift shafts,
walkways and garages. Death buzzes round that.

We set matches to paperbacks, cartons, copies
of *Time*. A pissy reek sharpens the smoke.
Outside, the towers of the Center shine,
electric constellations beyond the garbage swamp.
They've heat, light, power. We've the fire. Our goats,
red-eyed in the flames, chew mange into the carpet.

Here in the Burbs, we stitch a modest patchwork
of art, leisure, worship. Today, a Sunday,
we dedicate to baseball, prayer, and bird-singing
galas in the park. We bet which trills longest.
Dollar bills – a hundred buys a dented Heinz tin –
shuffle at the screams of the luminescent parrots.

Our orange-yellow-red mottled children flutter
in rings, chanting psalms of the Divine Messenger
Mercury: *Fat Bottomed Girls. Bohemian Rhapsody.*
We praise Him from the car park's topmost storey.
The high priest says unbolted bucket seats create
fine household altars. *Radio Ga Ga. Another One Bites.*

. . . And the Contraflow System Glittered

the hour the catalyst showered down, plating
  tarmac, slates and satellite dishes with electrum.
Pines in plantations straddling glens, Leylandii
  staking suburban gardens, ignited as needles
flared all at once. Nano-explosions, a trillion
  phosphorus fragments. Flyovers sparkled.
Concrete car parks wore diamonds.

  A hand had shaken nature's kaleidoscope;
the film-reel of every genome spliced
  into jump-cuts, the double helix unsprung.
People, too. Our retinas hardened into crystal.
  We felt brittle bulbs swivel in our skulls.
We saw shimmering purples once exclusive
  to fruit flies and privileged species of beetle.

A sky siren ululated, a stratospheric muezzin.
  We drifted from offices, flats and farms,
past quartz-encrusted traffic jams.
  Clouds extruded vapour stairways
a jet flight high. We left texts unwritten,
  tablets on. Shed organs, bones and skin.
In files of thousands began the climb.

Big Band Theory

Creation was our final number.
We bunched together on the stand,
tight as protons in the primeval atom.
Each beat the trombonist blew a low E
I felt a brass bend dig into my spine.

Gene Krupa's cymbals hissed like surf.
Saxes cried, wheeling round a headland.
I swear I saw the sea . . . But what *was* sea?
Come to that, what was water? Now
was the timeless time, before matter.

Yet the wave swung me, irresistibly.
I reared up the brass bell of my tenor –
Earl Hines yelled, *Ouch, you palooka!* –
and blew a hurricane of quarks in B flat.
Gene caught the beat, pushed us harder.

Earl joined in with modal runs. Quavers
from his wah-wah jumped between quanta;
swinging electrons. Glenn Miller conducted
faster and faster, became a blur,
his baton a hair in Van De Graaff generator,

till he gave up and tossed it into space –
that I saw *was* space, billowing into being,
a solo blown from a horn – and Jesus Buddha,
Everything was born. Gene screamed, *All right!*
Stars. Light. Earl sang the first Hallelujah.

Sundowner

Around five, when the Polish girl touches my elbow
to lead me downstairs to eat, the curtains ignite
like the Messerschmitt I saw shot down.
Struts exposed, ribs of a sizzling carcass.
A hot turpentine wash as the drop tank explodes.
The pilot dangles from his chute five fields away,
an exclamation mark punctuating the sky.

I assemble the memory. It comes in prefab parts
whose tapering extrusions grip the frame;
an Airfix kit I stick together, tailplane, fuselage,
cannon. If my eyes could cope I'd find my old
darning tin, unravel a thread, hang the model,
tap it so it twists. Evasive action. But cataracts
shrivel the world. Residue flakes off a dry seam.

I see the corpse of glue. Still, this evening,
when the sun crashes into room 302,
I teeter on the cockpit's lip, bail out
and fly, leaving the shell to fry in kerosene.
Halfway from heaven, I watch the horizon
yaw and right itself, the silk dome fill.
The Polish girl screams, a plunging engine.

Endpapers

Whenever I shape to say *For God's sake*
just end it, my words panic in shoals,
fleeing hammerheads and great whites
of proper nouns that snap whenever
an abstract swims past: love, memory,
attachment, charm. *She published over thirty*
historical romances, says the boy who carries
my marble eyes, piggy-pink cheeks,
the nose I inherited from a Persian envoy
in a Christian bed . . . it's a four-book saga.

My father, bastard son of the Ambassador,
floats at the boy's shoulder, crooking
a translucent finger. I want to rise,
now – shred this veil of ironed sheets
and soar beside him through the window,
across the grounds, above the breeze-bent
ash copse and beyond the Home – jet streams,
eagles, boiling clouds! *Let's just lie down,*
Mother, says piggy boy, pressing me
gently as a rose petal onto paper.

Paperbacks bubble off the shelf and float.
My tenth novel dives into the commode.
The doctor hems, unfolds a paper. *So just*
this concluding form. Father shines now,
arms wide as trees. *I'm sorry,* says the boy
with rheumy eyes, *I can't bring myself to sign.*
Doctor shrugs. Father's gone. My sentences
whisper a tired tale. A wrinkled Scheherazade
postpones the needle. But I trawl a weighted
breath, fish out one thrashing syllable: *Please.*

Worlds

The long day wanes: the slow moon climbs: the deep
Moans round with many voices. Come, my friends,
'Tis not too late to seek a newer world.
Push off, and sitting well in order smite
The sounding furrows; for my purpose holds
To sail beyond the sunset, and the baths
Of all the western stars, until I die.

Tennyson, *Ulysses*

World of Bones

Our first impression? A labyrinth of skeletons. The sentient native species had fashioned animal bones into a city. Stairways hacked from vertebrae, ribcage apartments, a washing line improvised from the radius and ulna of an albatross wing. Carnivorous insects and carrion birds plucked at the bodies of dying organisms even before hearts and lungs stopped pumping, to speed the process of building. Only when all flesh had gone – either eaten away or left to drop into the dark interior far beneath the white hollow halls – did the natives move in.

A pyramid of elephant skulls formed the city's holiest building. A cathedral to a deity the natives called The Architect, or She Who Builds Ascension from the Static Empty. Their faith had no hallowed book or oral tradition. They told our contact team all the bones were signs, so they dwelt perpetually in The Architect's sacred writing.

Our diplomat, who volunteered to spend a year on this world of skeletons, was a musician. She aimed to charm the aliens using flutes and drumsticks carved from surplus bones. Indeed, on our return, we felt the whole planet shudder with song. Through gaps between ribs, the wind whistled a hymn. Fibulae, suspended as chimes, tinkled. Ear-bones rattled in rhythm. Our envoy sat enthroned at the pyramid's apex. The natives said, *Kneel on that coccyx. Praise her.*

World of Levels

This planet presented unique problems to the survey team sent to draw maps. Its surface could only be represented in three dimensions, as each plate of the crust supported a series of gradually smaller planes on vast pillars of a crystalline allotrope of silicon.

One surveyor imagined the planet a paradise left by departed kings, a Hanging Gardens of Babylon. And at first glance the myth was apposite enough. Viewed from space, the layered planes tessellated in geometric patterns, fired in fierce reds and golds as dawn traversed the surface. The rivers ended in spectacular waterfalls that tumbled off each edge onto the plane below with a force of billions of Newtons. Yet the crust showed no trace of erosion, as if the system had never known the crack, crumble, crash and reconstruction common to all land on Earth.

As we modelled the surface in hologram, we saw a world founded on intricate repetition. Animals like zebras migrated across savannahs. The herds followed elaborate trails that would only recur every ninety turns of the planet around its sun – or so our data projections claimed. Surely such a number could not be random. Yet what intelligence would fashion a world as a clockwork repeating machine and then abscond? One comedian on the survey team dubbed the planet a huge graffito, and used a light-pen to scrawl across the hologram, *Builders Were Here*.

World Without Destinations

Roundabouts, flyovers and roads covered every square mile of the planet's surface. The indigenous aliens had developed a religion based on motion. A scream in a switchback car was, to them, a psalm. A jogger's pant, a mantra. Concrete half pipes formed roadside shrines where acolytes would leap from speeding vehicles to execute loops for hours, sometimes whole days, on specially consecrated motorized skateboards.

To avoid offending the indigenes we stamped, shuffled and danced when we spoke to them, even joined in the occasional recreational run, but our hearts pumped too sluggishly to confirm enthusiasm. We were disqualified, condemned on one occasion to the treadmills of the energy generating prison. We made whispered contact with the inmates, dissidents who stayed in one spot for entire seconds and covertly practised Zen.

Our video technician took to filming the pachinko agitation of the busiest intersections, zooming out to encompass the perpetual contraflow of the concrete overpass system, then panning up into the clouds as if vapour condensed then let loose from its moorings to drift across continents could offer a silent yet eloquent alternative to those hectic epiphanies promised by the Church of Kinetic Ecstasy.

World at the Edge

We steered the *Proteus* as near as we dared to the vast black hole at the galactic centre. There, straddling the event horizon, the line where space-time turns opaque and folds in on itself, hovered the World at the Edge. All its particles leapt perpetually between quantum levels. One jump too far could topple any electron inward, to fall into the hole forever, or outward, surfing a wave of Hawking radiation across the universe. Consequently, the inhabitants presented fuzzy outlines. Their bodies shimmered at the margins, teetering on a subatomic fulcrum between here, now and nowhere.

They hailed us with a rain of questions: *Why are you so simple? The motion of your limbs appears sluggish, handicapped by inertia, as if you are straitjacketed in a static configuration and lack the event horizon's perpetually vibrating ambiguous motion. Yet we acknowledge our own ignorance. The lip of a black hole is hardly a place to acquire definitive knowledge of universal laws. Therefore tell us. What are you? How do you live without the constant awareness that at any time a random cluster of your quarks may disappear?*

Easy, replied our ship's chaplain. *Our consistency is mere illusion. We tread the margin of the singularity at every moment. Only habit, hardest prison to break, keeps us from seeing the dark.* He stole a shuttle before we could stop him, launched it at the hole and imploded into nothing. The People of the Edge forwarded his final koan: *I trace the curve between empty space and the no-space empty of emptiness. I travel yet have always arrived. What am I?*

World of Disposable Forms

This planet advertised itself even to the outermost margins of its solar system. Brassy slogans blared on the twenty-one-centimetre hydrogen wavelength understood by every civilization with radio communication. Yet along each vector of reception, the signals dropped rapidly in frequency. This simulated red shift fomented the fear that the planet, with all its bodies on time-limited discounts, was perpetually receding beyond the grasp of any buyer who did not act without delay.

Here, said the radio pulses, *is the spine, liver and heart you have always pined for. Your quest for new skin is over. Choose from our unrivalled cornucopia of somatic templates, awaiting only customization to your unique requirements, then simply upload your mind.* The planet's executive cadres saw thoughts, memories and dreams as data to cram into the substrate slotted into the brain (or root bowl or cell nucleus or pseudopodia) of whatever organic structure the customer desired for her next incarnation.

Human Resources announced their decision to leave our ship and become a termite hive. One middle manager, our captain's former partner, messaged him thus: *I am reborn as two thousand four hundred and ninety-nine warriors. A toxic alkaloid is our chief weapon, injected from a segmented and flexible sting superior to that of the scorpion. In massing to attack at the queen's command, I know at last my calling. Join me, darling.* As the captain triggered the lift-off sequence, his nictitating membrane flicked aside a vestigial mammalian tear.

Message Never Received

Yesterday London brushed the penumbra of a total solar eclipse. The sky turned grey as dishwater. The sleeping hairs on my sleeveless arms awoke. The shadow of our cherry tree purpled like a bruise. The sun was a nail cresting the fingertip of the moon. We endure one such darkening every handful of years, when one body passes between Earth and another.

That's my way of telling you I've found a new lover. You'll never return in my lifetime, and if by some chicanery of science you do, you'll find me clutching pebbles in gritty fists, grasping bladdered ropes of wrack on the shore of senility, about to slip into the sea. I want to drown. I don't want to dwell any more on the flickering artificial star I saw through my telescope; the *Proteus* passing Mars, a boat on an ocean of nothing.

Of course, space is never entirely void of matter. Loose electrons, asteroids free of solar systems, even the amino acid blueprints of life forms, all drift between suns. That's how the biosphere began. We're descended from travelling dust. So your wanderlust is regression to archetype, my voyager.

Tonight I'll pick a star at random, decide it's you, set my compass by it and reorientate my world. I'll sail West to China, North to the Cape of Good Hope. And I'll arrive eventually, because Earth, my prison, is a sphere. Or will it have warped into a new figure I never imagined? A rollercoaster or Mobius strip?

This is hardly a message from your wife, then. It's a Rorschach stain. The sender of this file does not exist. It's mere light. A flash, a pattern. Part of the interstellar flotsam it reflects on. The stars in this galaxy outnumber English words. By three hundred thousand to one.

Reply Never Sent

At eighty percent of the speed of light, time slows down. Years, decades, centuries echo between heartbeats. A ship-year might last a whole generation on Earth, might let an ice age pass, might rearrange continents. Yet I am escaping too fast from you. I have become a beam of energy. Am I particle or wave? Either, depending on who observes me. I can pulse, scatter, bend around suns. I am the medium through which you look into the cosmos, seen in shapes of millennia ago, because any space is a moment-space whose hyphen matters more than either word.

Distance is time flown. By the time you read this the ice caps will have melted then frozen again, the glaciers dissected Europe. Silicon chips will sleep in glass cases, inert as mummies. As you finish this message you too will be light. Your particles will tremble in glass. Your waves will sink into night pools, the polished armour of solar panels.

Perhaps photons are individuals with signatures that scanners cannot measure. So when our beams overlap and generate an interference pattern, will you recognize mine? Will I know the source of yours? A white-hot filament, a spark bolting through a tube of noble gas, a nugget of carbon sifted from the core of a long-exhausted star?

Spiral World

Some gifted but perverse demiurge had drawn a seashell on space and crowded its exterior with mountains, forests, rivers and seas. The planet defied gravity with its forever tightening curve, its warped cylindrical crust. It had no core, but formed a hollow ram's horn wrapped around itself.

Over centuries the sentient native species had perfected their favourite sport. A drill would bore a hole in the shell and then the player, harnessed to a cable hundreds of miles long, would leap into the empty centre of the tunnel.

Depending on the diameter of the cylinder, the fall could last up to ninety-six minutes. Limbs stretched into an X, the player would fix her gaze on the inner surface of the shell, hoping to catch a glimpse of a jumper from the opposite face.

Some virtuosos of the game arranged to meet in mid-fall, lock hands and dance against the wrench of the spiral planet's eccentric spin. Head-mounted cameras captured these ballets for TV. *We are empty,* sang the theme song for the highlights show, *but we thread the spiral as we fall. We are free.*

World Without Coloured Bodies

Chromosome, our envoy explained to the native scientific colloquium, *derives from the language of the Ancient Greeks – a seafaring tribe of many gods, partial to myths, monsters, labyrinths and wars – and translates literally as coloured body.* The aliens smiled at his presumption, explaining that helical strands, carrying information inherited at random, formed an absurdly unfeasible basis for evolution.

Their own genetics were far more elegant. Traits were passed on wholesale to each new generation and blended. Thus difference gradually disappeared. Grey was the universal skin colour. All hair was black. Racism, tongue rolling, earlobes and warfare were unknown. Their eyes were the blue of the planet's admittedly beautiful skies, whose jostling, varied clouds defied the uniformity of the clone species below.

My indigenous lover, whom I identified by a blemish on the upper left thigh, suggested we defy the odds of inter-species infertility and risk a baby. Our child might revert to the grey-black uniformity of its native parent, or favour my red curls and star-cluster freckles. Our planned experiment proved redundant when our warp navigation officer gave birth to quadruplets whose hair flashed from black to her own blonde at intervals of eighteen milliseconds. DNA slides taken from these boy-girls (for sex also oscillated), did not show double strands intertwined, but a flickering fractal rainbow.

We left two twins below and took the other pair up into the *Proteus,* unsure which were the luckier; the shifting oddities defying a uniform world, or the pair whose shimmer merely mimicked the stutter of cellular programs executing routines; the stream of machine code in our activating genes.

World of Cyclic Fire

The planet's atmosphere held fractionally more than twenty-four percent oxygen. Enough to ensure no flame ever died but would hiss and creep and spit out sparks as it hunted fresh carbon. A continuous belt of fire tore across the landmass as if racing the sun. Three miles wide, it caught up with its own ash every hundred and nineteen years.

Life presented severe challenges to the few species determined to evolve in such conditions. One tribe dynamited an enormous basin out of rock, flooded it and spent generations developing swim bladders, scales, fins. They forgot gills, which had in the end to be cloned in a prefabricated laboratory erected and dismantled every cycle as the fire approached. Another tribe emigrated to the planet's ice cap. Their intellectuals built a university on the brink of the polar shelf. Unfortunately, entire faculties were submerged as bergs calved off, drifted into water warmed by the fire's passage and promptly melted. Meteorology was drowned in one such calving, rendering the people unable to gauge the weather.

Their religion deserves special comment. A mystic known only as The Flyer sewed an enormous sack from rhino hides, leaving a hole at the bottom. He carved a slender bowl out of rock and hung it from chains below the hole. He rode his balloon above the cycling flames, perpetually suspended between the fire and the cold of the stratosphere. He became a medium between the indigenous tribes and the divine inferno. He would toss down stones carved with cryptic lines the people took for runes in the script of the flames. *The Flyer circles the world and speaks for the fire,* they informed our contact team. *He says it is fitting that every cycle our bones must crumble into powder. He says the fire cremates us so our ash can enrich the earth again.*

Déjà Entendu

All night, the motorway lays down overdubs. First a low continuous hiss, like the skull's blood heard in a shell. Then a rising drone as taxi drivers and policemen on overtime accelerate. Pipes, pallets, road cones, stacks of junk and tools shudder on the backs of trucks. There's a bang like shunting buffers. Rusty squeaks at irregular intervals announce the road is birthing an unprecedented species, a fusion of driver and car.

It's this layered song that will draw you back, husband. You'll sail home for the motorway's voiceless chorus that underpins the car alarms and owls. The current the police sirens float upon. The murmur that frets visitors awake but grants me permission to dream.

And I dream we're atoms again. Exothermic, fusing, covalent. All our reactions generate heat. Gravity, strong nuclear, weak nuclear, electromagnetism: forces we can't comprehend but dimly discern relations between, like cavemen seeing lightning smash the sky's skull and fearing angry demons.

Your genes are scraps of litter in a street. Mine? Grains flicked across a beach. We're paper and sand. Yet our words are photons fizzing between quantum states, waves of tiny but distinct amplitude splitting space. Threads of light. Beams that bind stars.

World of Doors

Portals, gateways, arches, barbicans, screens of plastic strips tacked up on drawing pins – this planet offered all manner of entrances, always abutting still more entrances, till those few sentient beings bent on travelling found themselves perpetually crossing thresholds, greeted by strangers they had sometimes always known. *One cannot pass beneath the same arch twice*, said their principal philosopher. *We evolve faster than the doors we build.*

Even the range called Sierra of the High Snows consisted of nothing but passes and ravines, with paper screens standing in for mountains. We travelled eleven days there on mules roped together, led by a native guide drawn from an elite corps trained for danger at high altitude. Brewing tea in a kettle hung on chains above our fire, he spat a stream of the juice of an intoxicating berry and stated, with slow portentous sagacity, *Mountains are entryways. The true climb is up the North Face of the Mind.* Eagerly we lifted a microphone to his lips, hoping to record yet greater wisdom, but that evening he slipped, drunk, off our trail and tore a paper mountain open.

We voted unanimously to press on. Our way crossed a bridge over a canyon full of intricate layers of lower bridges in a criss-cross pattern descending as far as the naked eye could see. Our old wooden bridge keened in the wind. Frayed suspension ropes undulated like spines of a lizard slithering across uneven ground. Footboards bucked in the slightest breeze. We took our first tentative steps towards the iron portcullis on the far side, hoping if any member of our party crossed alive, the sentries would take pity and admit one additional soul to the succeeding threshold.

Underworld

Our scanners declared the planet hollow. From orbit it looked leathery as geriatric skin, its craters dark as liver spots, wrapped in frayed bandages of cloud as if a priestly caste had mummified a pharaoh's head and sent it into space.

The fissure interested us most. A rift valley long as a continent but only a dozen miles thin, as if a fontanelle had failed to fuse as a newborn baby grew into an infant. We eased the shuttle down, ready for the empty centre of the world. The fissure's walls were holed with caves. We chose one at random and walked in.

A comet like a tracer bullet shot through us. We floated in a planet-sized, three-dimensional map of the galaxy. I soon found Earth. The parchment of the Sahara. The lit-up cities of India, fierce as supernovas. The opposite coasts seemed to fit together: Canada and Portugal, Brazil and the bight of Africa. Once a single landmass, split by continental drift. I felt my memories of space ease away at an equally unhurried, tectonic pace, driven by deep currents the crust could never comprehend. Gradually I zoomed in. Europe, Britain, London, home.

* * *

Blossom flecks the lawn beneath our cherry tree. My wife sits reading, twirling a helix of hair round a finger. She frowns at her magazine. *Scientific American.* The cover, crammed with spheres in primary colours. Atoms in a DNA molecule. A hollow spiral stair composed of tiny worlds.

Notes

The Steve Lay epigraph, quoted with permission, comes from his blog at http://blog.questionmark.com. Other epigraphs are taken from Project Gutenburg; www.gutenburg.org.

Hokusai's Rooster. Based on an incident related in W. Scott Morton, *Japan: Its History and Culture* (Crowell, 1970).

I Just Can't Help Believing. Elvis's decision to burn his library on New Age mysticism is described in Lisa Marie Presley and Priscilla Beaulieu Presley, *Elvis by the Presleys,* ed. David Ritz (Arrow, 2006).

Invisible Towns. This sequence imitates Italo Calvino's *Invisible Cities* (*Le città invisibili,* Einaudi, 1972); first English publication, trans. William Weaver (Secker and Warburg, 1974).

Odham's Colour Library of Knowledge. This was a children's encyclopaedia (Hamlyn, 1970). The titles of several volumes within the series are used in the poem.

Turbo Diesel Injection. The description of Kundalini as 'serpent of light and liquid fire' can be found on several websites, including themystica.com, experienceproject.com and loveenergetics.com.

LIVE CANON